FOREWORD

As important as oxygen is to living things. So also, is getting value for money and purchase of safe products is to every consumer. Whenever this all-important livewire is tampered with. The consumer is exposed to myriad of dangers such as loss of time, money, purchase of injurious products and health challenges.

Having you ever thought of why people stick to a product, service or brand? Even where we have other competing brands? The answer is not far-fetched. This is because the consumer purchased products that meet their specification and yearnings.

The market of nowadays is a highly competitive one, it is important to see the need to maintain a positive relationship with customers. The world has gone past the era of developing amazing products only, as consumers are not just interested in what you are selling, but on how you are selling and to a large extent what happens after you have sold to them. This shift shows that consumers have higher expectations for consumer service. This presents a great challenge for any business that will thrive. Creating an excellent customer experience that's consistent across every interaction is not negotiable in this regard. It is essential for consumers to have information on their fingertips regarding any products or services before they attempt to buy.

There is the need to plan, make a shopping list and decide on quality in order to have value for money.

The book is a guide on how to be a smart consumer in our ever-changing world. It discusses shopping as a thoughtful adventure that involves negotiation, scanning various markets and searching for the best products leading to an informed purchase. Avenues for redress whenever complain arises was also discussed.

CONTENTS

SMART CONSUMERS

'' A brand is no longer what we tell the consumers it is. It is what consumers tell each other it is. Scott Cook''.

INTRODUCTION

CHAPTER ONE

WHO IS A CONSUMER?

Consumers are people or business entities that purchase products or services. Consumers do not sell any item that they purchase.

They are the end users in the chain of distribution of goods and services. sometimes the consumer might not be the buyer. There is a thin line that separates **customers** from **consumers.** The customers buy the products and services but may end up not using them. But consumers are the ones who make use of the purchased products and services.

An example are young children who are end users of toys and games but their parents buy them. As such, in the market for toys, the buyer and consumers are different people. The goods we buy for our use are referred to as **consumer goods.** They are not bought for sales.

TYPES OF CONSUMERS

Consumers are divided into three major types based according to the nature of consumption.

> **DIRECT CONSUMERS**

These are the set of consumers for consumes what they prepare directly. They are also referred to as direct producers The basic needs of shelter, food and clothing are provided and used directly by these consumers for their own consumption. This occurred during the early period of civilization in the history of mankind.

➢ **SEASONAL CONSUMERS**

Seasonal consumers purchase goods and services on a seasonal basis. Their purchases are driven by season. They only shop when need arises and at certain period or time of the year. Any business selling seasonal products or offering seasonal services may have difficulty when they are out of season. There may be a long period of year without sales. Examples of products that are consumed on a seasonal basis are as follows;

➢ Umbrellas

➢ Summer clothes such as beach wears

➢ Rain coats during the rainy season

➢ Coffee or hot drinks during cold weather

➢ Cold drinks during hot weather

➢ **PERSONAL CONSUMERS**

Personal consumers buy what will be consumed by them or their family members. These are individual consumers who purchase goods solely for their family, house hold or personal use. Examples of products purchased by personal consumers are as follows;

Cars to be used personally, mobile phones for personal communication, personal clothes and other individual and household items.

> **ORGANIZATIONAL CONSUMERS**

Consumers at the organizational level purchase products for organization, businesses and governments. They purchase in bulk and place long term orders. As a result, they are highly priced, valued and sought after. There are established strict standards that need to be adhered to in selling to organizational consumers. Sometimes goods and services may be offered to these set of consumers at a negotiated price. Flexibility in negotiating price and rigidity in quality is key in dealing with organizational consumers.

> **IMPULSE BUYERS OF CONSUMERS**

These are consumers who buy on impulse as the name implies. Impulse buyers make purchase without planning. They make decision to purchase whenever they like or connect with products and services. The products and services are not within their plans. It is the appeal that makes them to purchase the products. Examples of such products are as follows;

Brightly coloured children toys, chocolates at supermarket checkout counters, cookies at customers' eye levels at the shelf etc.

> **CONSUMERS BY BARTER**

These set of consumers offer what they have in exchange for what others want. This arrangement is referred to as trade by barter. For example, a man who want corn for his family and has a goat must look for another person who has a corn to exchange for his goat.

> **MODERN CONSUMERS**

These are consumers who makes purchases with only money as a means of exchange for goods and services.

> **NEED BASED CONSUMERS**

Need based consumers only make purchases of items needed per time and not any other time. A need for a certain product or services will make it necessary for it to be bought almost immediately. An urgent need for a product and service need to be created by marketers in order to promote sale of products and services. Examples are fan, air-conditioners during hot weather, heaters during cold weather, light bulbs for illumination and life insurance when we think it is essential to protect our loved ones in case of the demise of a breadwinner.

> **DISCOUNT CONSUMERS**

These set of consumers purchase goods and services primarily because of the discount. They do not purchase unless they receive information about discount. Discount consumers will rather buy at a discounted price rather than the full price. Coupons, stock take and gift cards are common with them.

> **HABITUAL CONSUMERS**

These consumers are the ones who feel compelled to make use of certain brands or products. Cigarettes, beer, cologne or deodorant fall into this category of products that are popular with habitual consumers. Habitual consumers do not mind how much their trusted brand is going for. So far the brand is available. They marketers a hard time to convince them before they can switch their loyalty to any other brand.

'' You've to make consumers smart. An e-portal does not sell products at cheaper rates, instead an offline shop sells it

at costlier price.'' Jack Ma. Founder Ali Baba.

CHAPTER TWO

CHARACTERISTICS OF SMART CONSUMERS

Shopping nowadays is totally different from what it used to be in time past. There is a section of the society that takes shopping seriously. Shopping for them is not just for fun. But it is a thoughtful adventure that involves negotiation, scanning various markets and searching for the best products leading to an informed purchase. A normal consumer is no different from an impulse buyer in that they make purchasing decision either by trial and error or product appeal. Smart consumers however, look for quality products at an affordable or their pre-determined price. They are not brand freaks. Smart consumers may prefer an affordable, unbranded or not so popular brand and good quality products to an expensive and popular brand. These consumers hunt for stores that have affordable or discounted offers and good quality products. They can otherwise be called consumers who have purchasing or buying intelligence. The following are the characteristics of smart consumers.

> **THEY ALWAYS WANT TO BUY PRODUCTS AT THE LOWEST PRICE.**

Smart consumers have an eye for lowest price while intending to buy products. When we have a cluster of smart consumers. They may form group to purchase in bulk in order to further reduce price.

> **A SMART CONSUMER IS AN EXPLORER.**

They constantly hunt for stores to keep them abreast product offers, prices, quality of products and new launches in different markets. These consumers have information on where and how to get good products and prices.

> **THEIR PURCHASE IS DISCOUNT DRIVEN.**

Smart consumers keep track of discount sales and plan their purchase to coincide with end of season sales. They may purchase Christmas season cloth in June when the price is still moderate. They do not always go with the trend because it appears expensive to them.

> **THEY WANT QUALITY PRODUCTS AT A REASONABLE PRICE.**

Smart consumers want to buy a good product within their purchasing limit. They believe that brands charge unreasonable price for a quality product which should be available at lesser price. As a result, they tend to scan the market for same categories of product brand at a lesser price but the same quality.

> **THEY WANT VALUE FOR EVERY AMOUNT OF MONEY SPEND.**

Spending must be translated into value. Any product or services that will not return maximum value for money can never catch their attention.

➢ **SMART CONSUMERS LIKE VARIETY.**

They like to comb through varieties of products before making the final decision to purchase. When they are about to buy a category of product. they prefer to check the same product across different market before making a final decision. This helps them to see the same products with distinct features and figure out the one that is closest to their specification.

➢ **THEY LIKE TO KNOW THE FEATURES OF A PRODUCT IN DETAIL.**

Smart consumers unlike any other consumers likes to learn about and understand product features, quality parameters and possess a great depth of product knowledge. They rely on family members, peers, market, internet, shop keepers and literatures for information on product features. They develop their own product as well as service evaluation based on the knowledge they have gathered. They constantly use this evaluation to arrive at purchasing decision.

➢ **INFORMATION SHARING.**

Smart consumers do not like to keep information to themselves. They love to share information about offers, markets and products. As such they become leaders of thought when it comes to purchase of products and services.

➢ **THEY DECIDE THE BEST SHOPPING TYPE OR MODE TO ADOPT PER TIME WHEN MAKING PURCHASING DECISION.**

To purchase means a lot of things to different consumers. But to smart consumers it connotes fulfillment of criteria such as quality, money, styling, appealing features among other things. The above criteria serve as a guide to the mode of shopping to adopt be it internet, supermarket, open, market, door step delivery etc. Smart consumers have the tendency of saving at least 20% of their personal or household expenditures from purchases across various types of products and services. It is highly expedient for businesses that intend to survive in this age to offer product with minimum price and quality in order to attract smart consumers who they can turn into loyal customers in no distant time.

'' Smart consumers should know what all the options are.''

Rick Steves.

CHAPTER THREE

TIPS ON BEING SMART CONSUMERS

It is better to err on the side of caution goes a wise saying. Very paramount to being a smart consumer are the important tips to be equipped with before any purchase is made. The vital aspect of this is planning. When there is adequate preparation before planning. It is easy to achieve the goal of every purchase.

IN SHOP PURCHASE

The following steps are important whenever in shop physical purchase is going to be made.

> **PLANNING.**

   Before you hit the shop or the supermarket to buy. Plan what you want to buy. It is not out of place to make a list. You need to use the concept of the 6 WHYS in this regard. It is important to ask yourself the following questions. What do I have? What do I need? When do I need the item? How will I use it? What quality or quantity do I need? and what to pay for the item? If you are able to appropriately answer these questions. All of these can be arranged into a checklist and finally a budget to serve as a shopping or buying guide. Then you can be assured of a smart and smooth shopping experience.

- **RESEARCH THE PRODUCT AND THE SELLER.**

  It is not out of place to ask family and friends for advice on their experience with the seller and the product you intend to buy or the service you are planning to use. The response will determine if the product can be bought or the seller gives guarantees good user experience.

- **CONDUCT A REVIEW OF PRODUCT TEST RESULT FROM CONSUMER EXPERTS AND PAST CONSUMERS' COMMENTS.**

  This will enhance a good consumer experience because response from consumer experts and past consumers will give an insight if the product is of good quality or otherwise.

- **PRICE COMPARISM.**

  Prices from different sellers should be compared. Different sellers have different prices for the same products and brands. It is smart to get quotes from a variety of sellers and compare them before committing to purchase from anyone of them.

- **BACKGROUND CHECKS ON SERVICE PROVIDERS.**

  It is essential to conduct background checks on service providers such as doctors, lawyers, pharmacist and other contractors in other to ascertain if they are licensed to practice or are registered to operate within your locality. This will save you the hassle of receiving services from unregistered practitioners and running afoul of the law.

- **MAKE A DETAILED LIST.**

  The list of items to be purchased should be handy before going out to buy anything. This should be arranged with location of the different stores and items within a particular supermarket. This will save time, organize your trip, prevent forgetting any item, backtracking and avoiding the purchase of items that you do not need.

> **DECIDE ON QUALITY.**

Make a decision on the type and quality you want in an item. In doing this, the following should be considered. How you will use an item and for how long? The appearance of the item and how to maintain it? Can the same article with the same or higher quality be gotten somewhere else at a lesser price?

> **TAKE TIME TO READ CONTRACT DOCUMENTS BEFORE AGREEING TO SIGN.**

It is important to understand the terms of a contract before signing. If the contract document appears lengthy or too technical to understand. It is not out of place to secure the services of experts before agreeing to sign. Signing a contract document in a hurry is never a smart move for any consumer.

ONLINE SHOPPING

The advent of online shopping has made buying and selling easier than it used to be. But making purchases online has its drawbacks. It is essential for every consumer who intends to be smart and not be caught in the web of online fraud to be wary of the source they are buying from. Here are some of the tips to smart and safe online purchase.

> **BE KNOWLEDGEABLE ENOUGH THAT BOTH FAKE AND QUALITY PRODUCTS EXIST ONLINE.**

You need to double check from various sources before you believe any claim of quality online. As the internet is full of opportunities and ease of shopping experience. It can also be a place of deceit, scam and fraud. The more you recognize the dual nature of the internet. The clearer you know it for what actually it is and what it is not. Then you will be able to decipher whether you are being scammed or not.

➢ **INVESTIGATE ANY CLAIM ONLINE ABOUT A PRODUCT OR SERVICE BEFORE YOU COMMIT TO BUYING.**

It is essential that as a smart consumer that you read and review information about products from different sources going ahead with purchasing them. The essence of the review is to establish if they have integrity and if their claim about the product or service is actually true.

➢ **PAY ATTENTION TO HOW YOUR DATA IS USED.**

The frequency of the data you supply online will determine how often you will receive targeted advertisement. But aside the information you provide. Other private information is being accessed from other sources. Kindly think twice whenever you are to answer online survey question that requires you to supply information such as phone number, birthdate, location, workplace etc. This private information can be used to link other private areas of the web for detailed and deeper information about you which if it gets to a wrong hand can portend grave danger.

➢ **CHECKING OF BROWSER SETTING.**

It is highly recommended that consumers check their browser settings while shopping online. It is essential to adjust it especially if you do not want your shopping history to be shared with anyone.

➢ **STAY INFORMED ON CHANGES ONLINE.**

There are incessant changes to privacy laws, user agreement and platform usage. No matter how well you trust the online platform you are using. It is not out of place to look out for changes and be abreast of new trends. It is possible to buy anything with just one click online. But it is the responsibility of any smart consumers to be informed about changes online in other to be on a safer side.

> **BE SPECIFIC ON WHAT YOU ARE BUYING.**

Carefully choose the item you are selecting for purchase online. Be clear on the colour, weight, specification and other details.

> **BE AWARE OF THE TOTAL PRICE YOU ARE PAYING FOR THE GOODS OR SERVICES.**

Most of the time the prices of the goods displayed online are the basic price excluding delivery, taxes and so on. Kindly note the total price before proceeding to checkout and payment confirmation.

> **TRACK YOUR ORDER.**

It is recommended that consumers make effort to track their orders. It is also important to read the refund policy and the delivery period attached to a particular product before purchasing it. Most online stores and service providers issue order tracking number to a product or service whenever an order is placed. This will help you to determine the movement of the shipment until it arrives your location. If the item is delivered late. You can decide to ask for a refund or cancel the order totally.

> **PRODUCT WARRANTY.**

Every smart consumer needs to read warranty claims on any product before ordering them. Which part of the product is covered by warranty and for how long?

THINGS TO DO AFTER PURCHASE

Being a smart consumer does not end before and during the purchase of an item or usage of a service. It continues after the product has been purchased or service subscription has been made. The essence is to ensure that better consumer experience is enhanced. Here are things a list of few things to do after purchase has been made.

> **ALL PAPERS THAT COMES WITH YOUR PURCHASE ARE IMPORTANT.**

It is essential and smart to keep all papers that you use in your purchase. Warranty documents, contracts, printed or written sales receipt, manuals etc. should be kept. These documents need to be kept safe in case any problem arises with the products. They will serve as evidence to prove your claim in case you need to seek redress.

> **FOLLOW INSTRUCTIONS IN THE OWNERS' MANUAL.**

Smart consumers need to read and follow product and service instruction. This is because the way a product or service is used may affect future warranty claims.

> **BE CONVERSANT WITH RETURN POLICY.**

It is expedient to read return policy on a particular product before such a product is purchased. When this is known and understood. It will enhance decision making on how many days are allowable to return a defective product from the time of purchase.

'' We never try to sell to dumb consumers. We try to sell to the smart consumer.

Matt Rutledge. Founder Woot.

CHAPTER FOUR

HOW TO IDENTIFY FAKE PRODUCTS

Whenever there is an original product. Counterfeit also exist. It is therefore incumbent on consumers to take their time to distinguish fake products from the original. Product counterfeiters nowadays take their time to ensure that the it is difficult to distinguish an original item from the fake ones. Consumers, especially the smart ones then need to be extra vigilant in order to spot the difference. This is important because the purchase of counterfeit products lead to loss of hard earned money, loss of lives and properties.

Below are some of the tips to identify fake products.

> **PRODUCT DESCRIPTION**

Going through item product description will go a long way to expose a fake product whenever a purchase is to be made. Carefully analyzing the description of a counterfeit product and comparing it with that of an original one will reveal inconsistency or a total lack of important description. This is an area that counterfeiters always neglect. It is always a rule for consumers who intend to be smart to check product description especially when they are in doubt of the seller or even the product.

➤ LABELLING

Closely related to product description is labelling. This is also important. Consumers should carefully check the label of any product they are intending to purchase with that of an original product. This may not be easy. But in this age of internet. The exact label of an original product can be carefully checked on the company's website. Information such as date of manufacture, best before/expiry dates, country of manufacture/origin and exact address of the manufacturer will be clearly and correctly written on an original product.

➤ CARELESS PACKAGING

Genuine products are not shabbily packaged. Good brands spend a lot on their packaging. This shows that whenever you are offered a shabbily packaged product that does not fit into the box, packaged with inferior plastic or sagging cardboard. It is sure that such is a counterfeit product.

➤ COUNTRY OF ORIGIN

A 2017 situation report on counterfeiting and piracy in the European Union conducted by Europol and EUIPO revealed that most of the fake products comes from China. The report estimated that 72% of the fake products found in Japan, USA and EU are exported from China. Nigeria is also not excluded from this list. Whenever you want to purchase any product always be wary of its country of origin before you buy it. Products with the inscription such as "for export only" are either outright counterfeit and are not fully compliant with the minimum product requirement set out by the national and international regulatory authorities.

> ### CONSUMERS' REVIEWS AND PROFILE OF THE SELLER

In this age of that online shopping is widespread. The webpage of online shops has review section on each item offered for sale. These reviews are replete with comments of consumers on the performance of the product. These comments can serve as a pointer to how good or otherwise a product is. Reviews on independent review platforms can also help online consumers to ascertain the authenticity of a seller as well as the product. Some online marketplace does not sell other people's brand. While others do. But the existence of an independent review platform will serve as a pointer to the origin of a product or seller. Any product without a traceable origin or credible review is almost likely a fake product.

> ### FRAUDULENT WEBSITES

Sometimes to find an affordable price for a product is difficult. In this case consumers tend to go for alternative options. This becomes more difficult for online shopping because consumers tend to go through third party websites who re-direct shoppers to their websites by reducing their own prices. A golden rule to follow is to look up the location of an unfamiliar website on Whois Lookup and scam adviser before committing to buying from them. If the address of a seller is not listed authenticated or has been left out that is enough to raise a suspicion. If there are grammatical errors in a website URL and the product information. This is a pointer that the website is fraudulent and that they are peddling counterfeit product.

➤ UNREASONABLE PRICE

A tell-tale sign of a fake product is that it costs like a quarter of the price of the original product. Inferior materials are used to create the look alike of the original products thereby costing next to nothing in producing and marketing them. The manufacture of these replicas put consumers at risk. Please take note that if the price of a product is way below market value, marketed by an independent seller and is up to 60-80% discounted. It is most likely a fake product.

➤ POOR QUALITY OF PRODUCTS

The quality of fake product is always suspicious. Since cheap and low quality alternatives are used instead of quality raw materials. The materials can be cheap glass, fake leather, tacky plastic, old cloth, used or refurbished parts in electronic gadgets and appliances. The containers shape and size can be different. If all these signs are present. It is mostly certain that the product is fake.

➤ CODE MISMATCH AND OMMISSIONS

Genuine producers print unique identification features such as codes, patent, trademark serial and model numbers on the packaging of their products. Interestingly, fake products either miss out on some of the information or copy them wrongly on their own product. it is important to crosscheck that information online especially when buying electronic items and appliances.

➤ NO CONTACT DETAILS

When a manufacturers' address, phone number, email or other traceable details are not printed on the products' packaging. This should be a cause for worry. A genuine manufacturer who always want repeat business will not leave out these all important details in its product packaging. So purchasing a product without any form of contact means that there is no way of contacting the company in case the product turns out to be a defective one. It is smart not to purchase such product.

> **INCOMPLETE OR MISSING ACCESSORIES**

When the accessories listed on the packaging of a product are incomplete or missing. It can only mean one or two things. It is either the product is fake or has been tampered with. It is essential to check all the accessories listed on the packaging of a product for completeness inside the store for completeness before purchasing them. If it is an online purchase. It is not out of place to make a video recording of the unboxing of the product as soon as it is delivered.

> **UNATHOURIZED CENTRES**

Certain manufacturers have approved centers where their products can be purchased. It is better to procure items at such centers instead of patronizing unapproved stores who may likely be peddling fake products or may not be able offer a redress incase the product becomes defective.

> **MOBILE AUTHENTICATION SERVICE**

Regulatory authorities have developed schemes to combat counterfeiting and faking of products. A case in point is the Mobile Authentication Service (MAS) developed by the National Agency for Food and Drugs Administration and Control (NAFDAC). The scheme is one of the many strategies for combating drug counterfeiting in Nigeria. It uses scratch codes and short messaging service (SMS) to ensure that consumers very the authenticity of drugs at the point of buying. A panel is scratched by the consumers on the drug which shows a unique one-time PIN. This is sent toll-free to a short code using any of the mobile phone network provider. The consumers receive a direct response in form of text message stating if the product is original or fake. This method is a bit fail safe because response is received directly from the manufacturers and this is monitored by the regulatory agency.

➤ **PRODUCT AUTHENTICATION MARK**

Product Authentication Mark (PAM) just like the mobile authentication service is another tool used by regulatory agencies to empower consumers to detect counterfeit products. This scheme developed by the Standards Organization of Nigeria (SON) is applicable to both imported and locally manufactured products. Any imported or locally manufactured product with this mark is adjudged to have fulfilled the requirement of the standard or specification of such product. PAM is to ensure traceability of imported and locally manufactured products. It is also meant to provide assurance to consumers on products and ensure that they get value for money.

''The police cannot protect consumers. People need to be more aware and educated about identity theft. You need to be a little bit wiser, a lit bit smarter and there is nothing wrong with being skeptical. We live in a time. When if you make it easy for someone to steal from you, someone will."

--Frank Abagnale...

CHAPTER FIVE

CONSUMER PROTECTION

CONSUMER RIGHTS

Consumers have rights which are inalienable and protected by the law. A lot of consumers are either not aware of them or do not know the right way to enforce it. Highlighted below are some of these rights protected by the law.

> Right to value of money: products and services should give value for money. The main aim of purchasing a product or subscribing to any service is to derive value and enjoy the worth of the payment made.

> Right to safety: products and services should not be hazardous or injurious to health. Usage of products and services should not cause bodily harm or hazard to the health of the users.

- ➤ Right to information: consumers have the right to be adequately informed about the services to which they are subscribing and the products being bought. Advertisement and product description should not confuse the consumers. They are protected under the law to be given the right information to make decision. Product description, labelling and advertisement should not be deceptive.

- ➤ Right to redress: consumers are entitled to redress when the products becomes either defective or the service becomes unsatisfactory.

- ➤ Right to choose: consumers should not be forced or cajoled to purchase any products. They should be able to freely make decision before purchasing any product or service.

- ➤ Consumer Education: consumers have the right to acquire information about the products.

- ➤ Right to representation: consumers have the inalienable right to be adequately represented where decisions about them was made. This include guidelines, procedures and standards. Whenever decisions are to be made about products and services.

Consumer complain channels and resolution

Every consumer has an inalienable right to complain whenever their satisfaction about a product or service is not met. No matter how careful we are. We might still have problem with purchased products once in a while. It is both our right and responsibility to complain. If we have genuine consumer issues. But the challenge is that most consumers seldom complains. They believe that complain usually goes through rigorous procedure that yields little result at the end.

Times are changing. Companies are becoming smarter. So are the consumers. Regulatory authorities are now more alive to their duties of mediating and enforcing standards in the area of fulfilling consumers' rights.

A problem cannot be solved if it is not reported.

STEPS TO TAKE IN FILLING A COMPLAIN

There are certain steps to take in order to ensure that a consumer complain is properly filed and gets the right result at the end of the day.

> **CONTACT THE SELLER**

The first thing to do whenever you have consumer issues is to contact the seller of the product. Most of the problem can be solved by contacting the sales person or representative that sold the product to you. If this does not work. It can be taken further by reaching out to the manufacturer or the headquarters of the company or organization.

Customer relations or consumer affairs division that exist in most organization are with the primary aim of solving consumer problems. Contact information about them are always written on product labels and contract agreement form.

Most companies' website has ''contact us'' on their pages. The form can also be used to file complain about any consumer issues.

> **REGULATORY AUTHORITIES**

Whenever you are not satisfied with the response of a seller to your complain. Do not give up. Once the seller has been given ample time to respond, consider filing a complaint with regulatory agencies.

The table below shows a few regulatory agencies that exist in Nigeria and their areas of operation as regards consumer complain resolution.

S/N	TYPE OF COMPLAIN	REGULATORY AGENCIES	WEBSITE
1.	Food and drug related issues	National Agency for Food and Drug Administration and Control (NAFDAC)	www.nafdac.gov.ng
2.	Electricity issues	Nigeria Electricity Regulatory Commission (NERC)	www.nerc.gov.ng
3.	Locally manufactured and	Standards	www.son.gov.ng

	imported consumer goods.	Organization of Nigeria (SON)	
4.	Banking related issues	Central Bank of Nigeria (CBN)	www.cbn.gov.ng cpd@cbn.gov.ng
5.	General service failure	Federal Competition and Consumer Complain Commission (FCCPC)	www.fccpc.gov.ng
6.	Telecommunication service issues	Nigeria Communication Commission (NCC)	www.ncc.gov.ng
7.	Airlines and flight disruption issues	Nigeria Civil Aviation Authority (NCAA)	www.ncaa.gov.ng

> **GOOD COMPLAIN STRATEGY**

Every smart consumer needs a good strategy so that their complain can be attended to and adequately resolved. The steps to be taken in order to achieve a good result are as follows;

- Calmly and accurately explain the problem to each person you contact. Let them know your exact demand. Do not allow emotions to short circuit the details of the problems.

- Document your communication with the company. It is beneficial to have your complain written down whether inform of a letter or an email.

- Be brief and straight to the point. Note all the important details about your purchase. This should include the name of the item, number of the item, serial or model number, name and location of the seller, and the time of purchase.

- State what you want the organization to do about the problem and how long you will be willing to wait for their response.

- Refrain from writing angry, sarcastic or threatening letter. Please note that the person reading your letter was not the person responsible for it. This might jeopardize your chance for a good resolution.

- Include all documents about the issue. Keep the originals with you.

- Provide your name, address, phone numbers, emails and account number. If account is involved.

- Your letter should be sent by certified mail or request delivery confirmation.

- If you use company online complain form. Take a screen shot or print out the page before you submit so that you can have a record of your complain.

> **SAMPLE COMPLAIN LETTER OR EMAIL ATTACHMENT**

Your   Address,

City,

Date

Contact Persons' Name,

Name of Company

Consumer Complaint Division

Address, City

Dear Contact Person,

   Re: (Account number if an account is involved),

On **(date)**, I **(bought, leased, rented, repaired or serviced, subscribe to)** a **(name the product or service with serial number, ticket number or service performed)** at **(location or important details of the transaction).**

Unfortunately, your **(product or service)** has not performed well **(or the service was inadequate)** because

(state the problem).

I am disappointed **(explain the problem: for example, the product does not work properly, the service was poorly rendered, I was overcharged or wrongly billed, something was not disclosed clearly or was misrepresented …..).**

To resolve the problem, I would appreciate if you would **(state the specific action you want-money back, repair, exchange, etc).** Enclosed are copies **(do not send originals)** of my records **(including receipts, guaranties, warranties, contracts, tickets, model or serial number …..).**

I look forward to your reply and a resolution to my problem and shall wait until **(set a reasonable time limit based on the seriousness of the problem)** before seeking help from a regulatory or consumer protection agency.

Please contact me at the address, email or phone number (**indicate your current contact details here).**

Yours Sincerely,

Your name

Enclosures

ABOUT THE BOOK

Shopping nowadays is totally different from what it used to be in time past. There is a section of the society that takes shopping seriously. Shopping for them is not just for fun. But it is a thoughtful adventure that involves negotiation, scanning various markets and searching for the best products leading to an informed purchase. A normal consumer is no different from an impulse buyer in that they make purchasing decision either by trial and error or product appeal. Smart consumers however, look for quality products at an affordable or their pre-determined price. The books is an attempt to dissect the requirement for being a smart consumer in our ever changing world. Chapter one describes who consumers are? Characteristics of smart consumers was discussed in chapter two. The focus of chapter three was tips on how to be a smart consumer.

Chapter four discussed how to identify fake products. While chapter five dwelled on consumer protection.

ABOUT THE AUTHOR

AJALA ABAYOMI ADENIYI

AJALA ABAYOMI ADENIYI is a technical writer, factory inspection team leader and lead auditor that specializes in quality factory inspection, quality management & food safety management system audits. He has over seven years' experience both as a consumer complain committee member and Quality Management Systems Client Manager. He is a PhD research fellow specializing in natural product Chemistry at Ladoke Akintola University of Technology (LAUTECH) Ogbomoso.

REFERENCES

1. www.usa.gov/complaint-letter

2. Consumer action handbook (2017): www.usa.gov.

3. United Nations Conference on Trade and Development (UNCTAD): United Nations Guidelines on consumer protection (2016).